SHAPES

illustrated by
Sue Hendra

WALKER BOOKS
AND SUBSIDIARIES

LONDON • BOSTON • SYDNEY

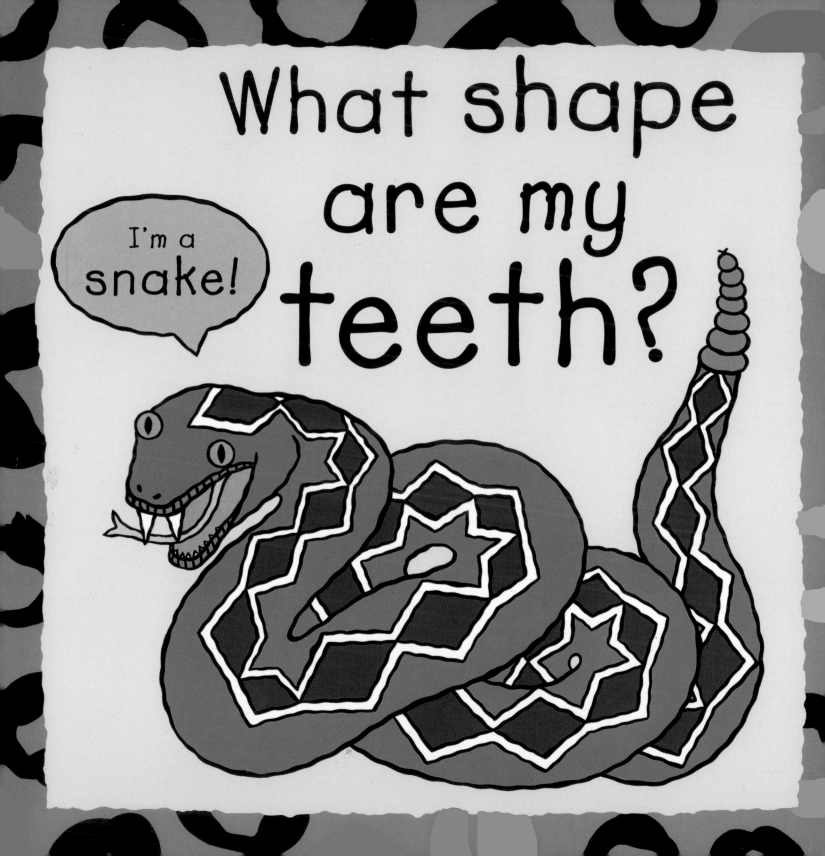

First published 2000 by Walker Books Ltd
87 Vauxhall Walk, London SE11 5HJ

2 4 6 8 10 9 7 5 3 1

Series concept and design by Louise Jackson

Words by Paul Harrison and Louise Jackson

Wildlife consultant: Martin Jenkins

This book has been typeset in Lemonade.

Printed in Singapore

British Library Cataloguing in Publication Data
A catalogue record for this book is available
from the British Library.

ISBN 0-7445-6254-6

circle

rectangle

triangle

oval

circle

star

oval

rectangle

triangle

circle

triangle

rectangle

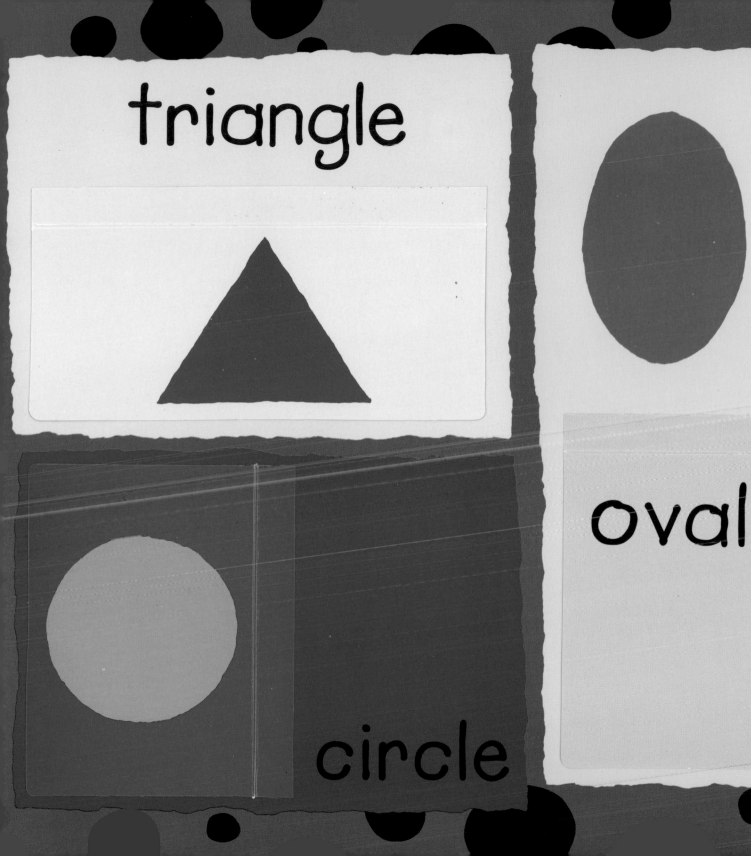

triangle

square

oval

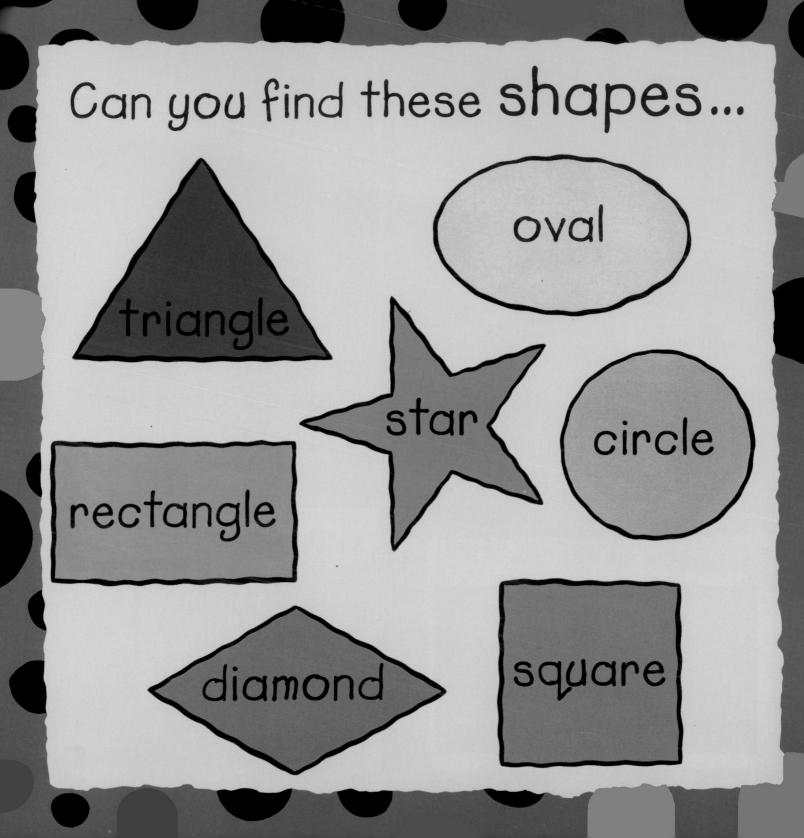

in these pictures?